Russia's Revival: Ambitions, Limitations, and Opportunities for the United States

Russia's Revival: Ambitions, Limitations, and Opportunities for the United States

By John W. Parker

Institute for National Strategic Studies
Strategic Perspectives, No. 3

Series Editor: Phillip C. Saunders

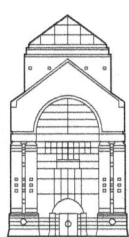

National Defense University Press
Washington, D.C.
January 2011

First printing, January 2011

For current publications of the Institute for National Strategic Studies, please go to the National Defense University Web site at: www.ndu.edu/inss.

Contents

Executive Summary

Independent Russia is approaching the start of its third decade of post-Soviet existence. After the economic chaos of the Boris Yeltsin decade and the recovery and stabilization of the Vladimir Putin decade, Russia's leaders have high ambitions for a return to great power status in the years ahead. Their aspirations are tempered, however, by the realities of Russia's social, economic, and military shortcomings and vulnerabilities, laid painfully bare by the stress test of the recent global financial crisis. Looking ahead, some also calculate that Russia will be increasingly challenged in the Far East by a rising China and in the Middle East by an Iran that aspires to regional hegemony.

With energy riches abundant enough to compensate for a multitude of governance and managerial shortcomings, the Russian economy will likely continue to grow in absolute terms in the years ahead. Indeed, if Russia wants to remain a mediocre power, it can do so without effort by not changing its current behavior patterns. But with growing corruption, business-stifling political controls, and dependency on raw materials exports retarding the full potential of Russia's growth, the country is facing the prospect of decades of decline relative to other more dynamic regional and world powers.

Russia will retain its nuclear weapons and permanent veto-empowered seat in the United Nations Security Council. But Russia will likely slip on many of the measures commonly used to assess great power status: size and vitality of its population, growth and vibrancy of its economy, and the ability of its armed forces to project conventional military power beyond its own borders. Russia will continue to be the preponderant influence across a large swath of former Soviet territory, but not beyond it.

As a result, Moscow is already seeking to strengthen Russia's ties with Europe and the United States. The West is seen as crucial to Russia's modernization as well as a hedge against what may develop to Russia's east and south in coming decades. This process of Russia's anchoring itself more firmly in the West will proceed with lots of tactical hiccups and sporadic crises. Nevertheless, it will bring consequences and opportunities for U.S. diplomacy and strategic development, some of which the Barack Obama administration's policy of "reset" is already reaping. But Russian policy toward the United States is conditional on a U.S. approach that engages Russia in positive ways. If that policy were to change, it could push Russia and China closer together on some issues in an effort to constrain the United States.

Introduction

In February 2008, then-President Vladimir Putin unveiled his vision for Russia's development strategy to 2020, often referred to as "Russia 2020."[1] Guided by Putin's speech, the Ministry of Economic Development and Trade formulated ambitious plans to make Russia the fifth largest economy in the world after the United States, China, India, and Japan. Russia's gross domestic product (GDP) would expand an average 6.5 percent per year. Its share of the world GDP would increase from 2.5 percent to 4 percent. A national innovation system, competitive human capital, and regional development centers would boost Russia's per capita GDP from $12,000 to $30,000—that is, from the equivalent of a quarter of the U.S. average to half of it.[2]

Nearly 3 years later, in the wake of the global financial crisis, it is clear that achieving the goals of "Russia 2020" will be a stretch. The 2008–2009 crisis hit Russia especially hard, underscoring its vulnerabilities. Oil went from $145 a barrel in July 2008 to $36 in January 2009. In the decade leading up to the onset of the crisis, Russia's GDP had soared from $200 billion to $1.8 trillion, one of the fastest growth rates in the world. But in 2009, Russia's GDP fell by 7.9 percent, the largest drop of any of the Group of 20 (G–20) countries (the world's largest economies).[3] By fall 2010, according to one poll, the proportion of Russian citizens confident that Russia would return to superpower status within 10 to 15 years had dropped from 50 percent before the crisis to 36 percent.[4]

In 2010, even as the price of oil recovered to the $70–$80 per barrel range and continued to rise, Russia's GDP struggled to rebound and remains sluggish. The Ministry of Economic Development in September forecast 3.5 to 4 percent growth by the end of the year, but reported that the economy had actually contracted by 0.4 percent in both July and August; others now believe growth for the year will be closer to the 3 to 3.5 percent range.[5] Looking forward to 2011–2013, the ministry forecast annual growth between 3.9 percent and 4.5 percent, several percentage points short of "Russia 2020" growth targets. Moreover, the draft budgets for these years assume that oil will stay in the $76–$79 per barrel range, but even at that world market price, experts envision deficits whose state financing could lead to a serious rise in inflation.[6]

During the decade when Russia boomed financially, many began to describe it as an "energy superpower."[7] However, the factors that will prevent Russia from attaining superpower status in the years ahead also soared during this same decade: corruption, renationalization, top-down political controls, and dependency on raw materials exports, particular oil and gas. Yegor Gaidar, Russia's first post-Soviet prime minister, several years ago argued that the mid-1980s drop in world oil prices contributed to the oil-dependent Soviet Union's collapse. Although numerous other factors also played a role in its dissolution, some analysts now see similar vulnerabilities for a post-Soviet Russia that has become greatly dependent on high energy prices for its economic and political sustainability.[8]

While the collapse of Russia may not necessarily be in the cards, the deck is certainly stacked against it becoming a superpower by 2020, or by any other date in the foreseeable future, and perhaps of even remaining a great power in the years ahead. Russia will retain its nuclear weapons and permanent veto-empowered seat in the United Nations (UN) Security Council. But Russia will likely slip on many of the measures commonly used to assess great power status: size and vitality of its population, growth and vibrancy of its economy, and the ability of its armed forces to project conventional military power beyond its own borders.

Some key variables are trending in the negative direction, and they are going to be hard to reverse. To make Putin's 2020 targets, labor productivity would have to average over 9 percent per year in the next decade, surpassing even China's recent astounding productivity rates.[9] At the same time, Russia is not making the most of some areas where it still retains a strong hand—particularly efficient exploitation of its fabulous endowment of energy and other natural resources. Even if high oil prices continue, demography will constrain Russia's advancement. Moreover, the geographic advantages Moscow had during imperial and Soviet times, when it expanded in all directions against weak neighbors, are now vulnerabilities. Russia in the decades ahead will have to contend with newly dynamic and historically aggrieved direct or near neighbors, particularly China and Iran. Twenty years after the Soviet collapse, Moscow no longer fields a first-class military to protect its borders, and it is still too early to presume the success of current military reform efforts.

Russia will continue to be the preponderant influence across a large swath of former Soviet territory, but not beyond it. Russia's hard and soft power will reinforce each other in the "near abroad."[10] Georgia, though, may remain the only place where Russia might again risk using hard power against a fractious neighbor, as it did in August 2008. Meanwhile, the Muslim populations in Russia's North Caucasus and even the central Volga regions are susceptible to influence by Sunni money and extremist ideologies from abroad. In a civil war with no letup in sight, over 10,000 military and internal security personnel have died and 27,000 have been wounded in the North Caucasus since 1988. Counting civilians, total fatalities in the post-Soviet period could be as high as 100,000,[11] and some have speculated that if current trends continue, Russia will sooner or later "lose" these territories.[12] In the thinly populated Far East, a burgeoning China poses a largely unspoken challenge in the decades ahead and is already pouring investment money into Central Asia and the Caucasus. To the south, Iran is a rising power intent on becoming a nuclear player.

With energy riches so abundant that they make up for a multitude of governance and managerial shortcomings, the Russian economy will likely continue to grow in absolute terms in the years ahead. But with these shortcomings retarding the full potential of Russia's growth, the country is facing the prospect of decades of decline relative to other more dynamic and booming regional and world powers. This will constrain Russian political and military ambitions, which some in Moscow already realize. Russia's share of global economic output fell from 4.1 percent in 1992 to 3.3 percent in 2008. Relative to China, Russia slid over this same period from having a GDP that was roughly equal to China's to one that was less than a third (and is now close to just a quarter). Relative to the United States, Russia's GDP fell from 18 percent in 1992 to 16 percent in 2008.[13] It is no wonder that President Dmitry Medvedev has underscored—however rhetorically—the need for modernization, without which Russia will slip further out of the top tier of world powers.[14]

Russia's current trajectory, however, opens up multiple opportunities for U.S. diplomacy, some of which the Obama administration's policy of reset has already been able to tap. In fact, a strategic reorientation of Russian foreign policy toward greater cooperation with Europe and the United States already seems under way. It is driven mainly by the economic vulnerabilities exposed by the global financial crisis, the military and security shortcomings underscored by the recent war with Georgia, the relentless rise and growth of China, and the frustrations of dealing with an Iranian leadership intent on pursuing a nuclear weapons program and becoming the dominant power in the Persian Gulf and Middle East.

On the Chinese front, even though Russia and China tout their current "strategic partnership," the future is uncertain and often troubling for Russian strategic thinkers and policymakers. As a result, some in Moscow argue that, even while doing everything to maintain good relations with China now, it is already important for Russia to begin to cooperate more fully with the United States and Europe because of inevitable problems with China in the future. To Russia's south, Iran's nuclear ambitions and expanding influence in the Middle East are also nudging Moscow toward this same conclusion.

Putin's Record

When Putin outlined his goals for "Russia 2020," the average 6.5 percent annual economic growth that his economic planners formulated did not seem outlandish. It was well within the margins of the growth rates that Russia had achieved during Putin's years in power. From 1999 through 2007, after all, Russia had averaged 7 percent GDP growth per year. As mesmerizing as that rate was, however, it was deceiving, since it followed a decade of post-Soviet collapse and contraction. In actual fact, Russia's economy at the beginning of 2008 was probably only around 5 percent bigger than it had been in 1990 in constant 1990 prices.[15]

Nevertheless, Russia, or at least Moscow, in 2008 was far beyond the "Upper Volta with nuclear missiles" of Aleksandr Bovin's famous 1989 quip.[16] There had been great economic changes since the ruble collapse of 1998 thanks to the economic reforms of the early Putin years and subsequent high prices on world oil and gas markets. A tremendous amount of new money has coursed through the Russian economy, and a lot of people—even ordinary ones—were a lot better off than before. Unfortunately, a large portion of the profits from high hydrocarbon prices had gone into corruption and consumption rather than into dynamic infrastructure investment. A joke making the rounds asks, "What is the difference between the American dream and the Russian dream?" The punch line answers, "The American dream is how to earn a million. The Russian dream is how to spend a million."

All the same, a visitor to Moscow will be rightfully impressed by its glitter and growth since the Soviet collapse. Russia's capital added 1.75 million inhabitants from 1989 to 2006, an increase of 20 percent.[17] But beneath that glitter and beyond the capital lay infrastructure rot caused by pervasive corruption, shoddy governance, demographic decline, and the still undone Soviet legacy of production assets—factories and workers—plunked down in economically untenable places by central planning. All these factors are a drag on efficient growth, and the list of painful consequences is long and continuing: from the tragic sinking of the *Kursk* submarine at the beginning of the Putin era, to the many test failures of the Bulava SLBM, to Gazprom's reluctance to invest in new domestic fields and pipelines, to a clumsy war against tiny Georgia, to regions in the Far East that are emptying while China booms on the other side of the border, to smoke from peat bog and forest fires drifting across central Russia and threatening the health and welfare of the residents of Moscow and other cities.[18]

Moscow's glitter is the exception, not the trendsetter. In attracting those fleeing economic bust and social violence elsewhere, the capital's economic magnetism exacerbates the gap instead of smoothing out the disparities between the center and the periphery. Beyond Moscow, abandoned villages and shrinking towns are common.[19] In suborning local interests and plundering local resources, Putin's "vertical of power" is reportedly spawning autonomy movements even in a number of ethnic Russian regions, leading some observers to ponder whether the Russian Federation could collapse just as did the Soviet Union.[20]

Nevertheless, the stock market by 2008 had soared to 20 times its original size. Foreign investors helped by pouring money into a booming emerging market. The Reserve Fund (Oil Stabilization Fund) held $140 billion to hedge against a drop in oil prices, and the National

Welfare Fund held another $30 billion to help safeguard pensions. Moreover, Russia's growth during these years benefited more than just the rich and powerful. Real incomes and wages more than doubled and tripled. Cell phones became ubiquitous. Car ownership boomed. Real estate in Moscow went from $700 to $6,000 per square meter.[21] To a visitor it would seem that everyone in Moscow has a cell phone. They constantly check them, even in the subway. They pull them out upon landing at the new Domodedovo airport to let their rides know they are on the ground. They have computers and want to know not only a visitor's phone number but also his or her email and Skype addresses.[22] According to a recent survey, computer ownership has risen from 8 percent in 2001 to 52 percent in 2010, with 63 percent of computer owners using them to access the Internet.[23]

Analysts attribute over half of Russia's growth during the 1999–2008 decade to early economic reforms.[24] From 1992 to 1997, during the Yeltsin years, Russia underwent the largest privatization campaign in history. Then, from 1998 into 2002, from just before Putin's early brief premiership into his first term as president, Putin pushed through a thorough reform of the tax system, including introduction of a flat personal income tax of 13 percent. At the same time, Russia integrated into the world economy as its imports and especially exports surged. Exports now account for 33 percent of Russia's GDP. Even in 2008, the current account surplus was $113 billion, or 7.7 percent of GDP. Rising oil prices contributed to much of this trade surplus, but the share of oil and gas in Russia's exports actually fell from 90 percent in the Soviet Union's last years to 60 percent in 2008.[25]

But Russia's reform efforts, particularly in the oil sector, came to a screeching halt and then went into reverse in 2003 when Putin imprisoned Yukos oil company head Mikhail Khodorkovsky. Yukos had been Russia's most profitable privately held oil company. Its $35 billion market value at one time was more than half of the Russian Federation's budget. But Khodorkovsky also had political ambitions and little respect for Putin, flaunting his independence from and even rivalry with the president. His plans to sell a big chunk of Yukos to Exxon-Mobil or Chevron and to change tax legislation challenged Putin's vision of the state dominating Russia's energy and natural resources sector.

Since 2001, Putin had been reining in headstrong, overly independent political and economic players, beginning with "capitalist ministers" inside the Russian state's own structures. Yevgeny Adamov from MinAtom was his first victim in April 2001. Shortly afterward, Putin ousted Rem Vyakhirev as Gazprom's chief executive officer and replaced him with protégé Aleksey Miller. This was the beginning of the end of Gazprom's status as a "state within the state." That June, government representatives gained a majority on Gazprom's board for the first time. A year later, this majority made Dmitry Medvedev, deputy chief of the Presidential Administration, chairman of the board; this was the same Medvedev who in 2008 would succeed Putin as president.

The action was a model and a precursor for what the Putin regime had in store for other "strategic sectors" in coming years. Putin had a high interest in and knowledge of the oil and gas sector, and the move against Khodorkovsky accelerated the state takeover of the commanding heights of those sectors. Gazprom declared a monopoly on gas exports from Russia, forcing private producers to play exclusively by Gazprom rules. Foreign energy majors also had their positions in Russian joint ventures undermined. Finally, Putin's green light to regime insiders to cannibalize Yukos cemented in place a system of continuous clashes over lucrative resources for political and personal gain between competing elite groups with Kremlin ties.[26]

As the regime reinstituted state control of the oil industry, it weakened private ownership and the discipline of capital markets. Oil export taxes rose to fill state coffers, depriving oil companies of funds to reinvest in exploration, modernization, and expansion. Inefficiencies set in as state control grew to over 80 percent of gas production and to around 45 percent of oil production. The impact was quick and measurable. In 2005, oil production growth slowed. In 2008, it actually declined.[27]

The impact of these measures and trends was masked by the spectacular growth in world oil prices beginning in 2004. The windfall allowed Russia to keep posting growth rates averaging 7 percent per year. Pundits began referring to Russia as an "energy superpower." But inflation remained high at over 10 percent, corruption expanded, and the economy remained heavily dependent on raw materials exports, primarily hydrocarbons, minerals, and metals. Moreover, with these raw materials exports accounting for around 30 percent of Russia's GDP as world commodity prices skyrocketed, Russia's economy was particularly vulnerable to a collapse once the bubble burst.[28]

Medvedev's Challenge

When that collapse in world commodity prices finally came, it was spectacular: oil went from $145 a barrel in July 2008 to $36 in January 2009. With around 85 percent of its exports based on hydrocarbons and other raw commodities, Russia's trade balance and GDP took a huge hit. After a decade of averaging 7 percent growth, Russia's economy contracted 7.9 percent in 2009, the most of any G–20 country. With the system on the line, Russia's initial response in 2008 was "mostly adequate," according to experts. But as oil prices recovered in 2009, the impulse of many reverted to preserving the status quo of comfortable stagnation instead of engaging in the painful restructuring necessary for long-term gain.[29]

Indeed, if Russia wants to remain a mediocre power, it can do so without effort by not changing its current behavior patterns. With oil again trading over $80 a barrel, it will take enormous political energy and determination to go back and pick up the thread of the Putin reforms that stopped in 2003. After all, while Russia's foreign currency reserves dropped from $598 billion in August 2008 to $436 billion in March 2010, they were still the third largest in the world.[30]

All the same, there is probably an increasing if grudging understanding that reforms are necessary if Russia is to compete with the world's advanced economies. Medvedev and even Putin seem to realize that something needs to be done. There are strikingly common themes in Putin's call for an "innovation society" in February 2008 and Medvedev's call for "modernization" in November 2009. Medvedev has criticized Russia's reliance on oil and gas exports as "primitive," and his call for "modernization" is a sign that Russia's leadership is aware of the problem, although the solutions laid out to date are inadequate and the obstacles to achieving even these half-measures are enormous.[31]

The challenge is to overcome inertia, systemic impediments, and outright opposition, particularly if oil prices remain relatively high. Not surprisingly, there is a lot of skepticism that Medvedev can turn things around. Sixty-one percent of participants in one session of the St. Petersburg International Economic Forum in June this year foresaw a stagnation scenario for the next 2 to 5 years, and 55 percent see it for the next 10 years.[32] Some see Putin as a cynic who is playing the game about modernization, while Medvedev, who is 10 years younger, is a believer. According to this view, this is a huge age gap. In this analysis, whether Medvedev is reelected as president in 2012 will be important.[33]

For now, Medvedev continues to push forward. His speech to Russia's ambassadors on July 12, 2010, was a landmark. He explicitly pointed to the August 2008 Russian-Georgian war and the global financial crisis as having spurred the new course toward "modernization" and a "paradigm shift in international relations." According to Medvedev, "We need . . . special modernization alliances with our main international partners. . . . First and foremost with countries like Germany, France, Italy, the EU [European Union] as a whole, the United States of America."[34]

Even Medvedev's cheerleaders, however, concede that there have been no "cardinal" changes so far and that Medvedev's signing in July of a law expanding the powers of the Federal Security Service (FSB) was a dangerous "step back" from democratization and modernization. Medvedev is conducting a "silent war," insists Igor Yurgens, head of the Institute of Contemporary Development and coauthor of a widely publicized critique of Russia's capabilities.[35] But he faces "very significant forces in the country that don't want any liberalism, any modernization," as well as a "conformist" society for whom "today's seeming well-being is more important than what happens 5–7 years from now."[36]

Even though the Russian economy saw some growth again in 2010, the return to $70-plus oil has knocked substantial wind out of the modernizers' sails. A participant in the annual Valdai Club discussions in September 2010 reported that the "momentum for reform" had "dissipated" compared to 2009. One senior Russian official at the meetings noted that the oil price rebound had brought with it a return to "complacency" and a worsening of corruption back to its precrisis level.[37]

As a result, Russia may actually wind up with the worst of both worlds: with recovered oil prices undercutting reform efforts, and this in turn hobbling a return to precrisis growth rates, leading to more budget deficits and possibly setting the stage for a return to politically destabilizing high inflation rates. In fact, some critics have begun to suggest that the government, lacking any thought-through strategy for a return to growth, is now beginning to "pray" for a jump in oil prices back to $100 a barrel or higher as the only way out of an impending crisis.[38]

Demographic Determinism

Beyond politics and economic policy, the objective obstacles to Russia remaining a great power are formidable. Foremost among them is a starkly declining population. Just after the Soviet collapse, on January 1, 1992, Russia's population stood at an estimated 148.5 million. Seventeen years later, on January 1, 2009, it was down to 141.9 million, a drop of nearly 7 million, or close to 5 percent. In the last 16 years of the Soviet era, births outnumbered deaths by 11.4 million. In the first 16 years of post-Soviet Russia, deaths outnumbered births by 12.4 million. Only thanks to migration has the post-Soviet population loss been limited to just under 7 million rather than exceeding 12 million.[39]

Russia's population has been experiencing a catastrophic decline in health for almost half a century, with no letup in sight. According to a leading expert, "No country in the modern era—not even the AIDS-ravaged states of sub-Saharan Africa—has sustained health setbacks as severe as Russia's for such a very long stretch of time." Too much drinking, too many cigarettes, a bad diet, and poor health care have all contributed to the calamity. Life expectancy for a 15-year-old male in Russia in 2006 was lower than in Cambodia, Haiti, Rwanda, or Somalia. A typical 20-year-old Russian male in 2006 had a less than even chance of making it to age 65, lower than his counterparts in Nigeria or Kenya. For Russian males and females together, the U.S. Census Bureau has projected a lower life expectancy in 2025 than in Bolivia, East Timor, and even Pakistan.[40]

If Russia could count on high oil and gas prices to sustain its growth as a world power, then a declining population would not be a big tragedy since oil and gas extraction are not labor-intensive enterprises. However, if economic growth and national survival depend on getting beyond dependency on hydrocarbon income to achieving sustainable economic diversification, then Russia's demographic projections are disastrous. Russia will have an increasingly declining population with less and less human capital to act as an engine for diversification and economic growth.[41]

Responding to the looming crisis, then-President Putin in 2007 endorsed a "Concept of Demographic Policy to 2025." By 2015, Russia's population would stabilize at 142 to 143 million, and by 2025 rise to 145 million. Life expectancy would rise to 75 years in 2025, up from 66 years in 2006. The fertility rate would reach 1.95, 50 percent higher than in the pre-2007 period. However, professional demographers give Russia no chance of reaching these targets. According to Russia's own official projections, the population will drop another 5.5 million by 2025 to under 136 million. The United Nations Development Programme (UNDP) projects a range of 127 to 137 million in 2025, and 122 to 135 million in 2030. The U.S. Census Bureau estimates 128 million in 2025 and 124 million in 2030.[42]

For the decades ahead, Russia's population decline is inevitable. According to Russia's own official projections, by 2025 there will be only 6.4 million women in their twenties, the prime child-bearing years, 45 percent less than now. With a shrinking cohort of potential mothers, maternity rates would have to surge dramatically just to maintain already low birth totals. At the same time, Russia's working age population will decline 14 percent from 2009 to 2025, and the ratio of working to retired population will drop from 3 to 1 in 2010 to 1.9 to 1 by 2030.[43] A good immigration or migrant worker policy could alleviate the impact of these trends on Russia as well as smooth relations with its neighbors, but so far Russia does not have one.[44]

If U.S. Census Bureau projections are on target, Russia's population will have declined by some 20 million between 1990 and 2025. Its size will have dropped from sixth to twelfth in the world, and from 2.2 percent to 1.6 percent of projected total global population. Russia's working age population will fall even more sharply, according to UNDP projections. As a result, annual labor productivity increases in Russia will have to average 2 percent more than the rest of world just to maintain Russia's current share of global GDP in 2025.[45]

Price Paradox

Russia's reliance on raw materials exports makes the country's welfare highly vulnerable to the volatility of commodity prices on world markets. In 2007, oil and gas accounted for 18 percent of Russia's GDP, 61 percent of its exports, and about 50 percent of its federal revenues.[46] According to one study of the 1994 to 2009 time period, every 1 percent increase (or dip) in the price of oil contributed to a 0.46 percent rise (or decline) in Russia's GDP.[47] This made the drop in the price of oil from $145 per barrel in July 2008 to $36 in January 2009 a severe shock. But even that low price is historically high and there is no guarantee that oil will stay in the range of $70 to $80 per barrel.[48] Gas profits are similarly unpredictable. According to preliminary data, Gazprom sales to Europe fell from $65 billion in 2008 to $42 billion in 2009.[49] The shift to shale gas and other alternative energy resources in the years ahead will contribute to further uncertainty.

Even at today's relatively high prices, Russia's immense raw materials riches are unlikely in the long run to be able totally to counterbalance the country's spectacular demographic decline.[50] Indeed, rather than setting the stage for Russia to become a sustainable great power, they contribute to making its situation worse by undermining incentives to reform, invest, and diversify. As long as oil, metals, and mineral prices stay high, today's profits obscure Russia's real situation, spawn ever greater corruption, and lower the incentive for investments and reforms aimed at improving Russia's long-term prospects. Russia already needs substantial international investments in new fields to keep up current oil and gas output.[51]

Putin's "Russia 2020" plan from early 2008 was evidence of this cycle of complacency. The global financial crisis that followed soon shattered many illusions. But as oil prices recovered from their early 2009 lows, that impact proved temporary. As Medvedev put it in May 2010, "To be blunt, $140 a barrel—this would be a catastrophe for Russia, this would destroy all stimuli for development."[52]

What many have described as the "energy curse" wreaks havoc in several ways. It focuses public and private energies on reaping energy profits rather than investing in diversification and new and upgraded production facilities. It saps the leadership and population of their will to pursue reforms that may cause short-term hardships. And its immense boom-year profits foster extreme corruption and degradation of the business environment. One of the results, as Anders Aslund and Andrew Kuchins have noted, is that "Russia's public administration has proven itself too incompetent and corrupt to undertake major [infrastructure] projects." Paved roads are an especially sore issue. From 2000 to 2006, they increased only from 754,000 kilometers to 755,000 kilometers, and then at three times the cost as in the West.[53]

Finally, as welcome as today's return to comparatively high oil prices might be in Moscow, there is yet another way in which they may actually be a harbinger of Russia's further relative decline as a world power. China will be addressed later in this paper, but for now it is relevant to note that at least $80-a-barrel oil is partly due to booming China's need for energy to fuel its spectacular growth. But as long as China continues to boom, Russia's world standing will continue to slide unless it undertakes drastic reforms.

Corruption Complex

Major reforms will be difficult, however, because Russia's economy is seized up by corruption. It is not just an ancillary phenomenon that is present in other countries as well but is at the core of the political-economic system that has evolved in Russia today. Aleksandr Golts, a long-time observer of the Russian military-industrial complex, for example, estimates that 30 to 50 percent of the state money allocated for new armaments disappears into kickbacks.[54]

Sergei Guriev, head of Moscow's Russian Economic School, argues that corruption is the "key problem of the Russian economy." Guriev points out that there can be "real achievements in the fight against corruption only when we have political competition, accountability of power, and transparency of governance."[55] The odds against this happening, however, are underscored by another joke recently making the rounds: after several days of deliberation, the Constitutional Court of the Russian Federation declared that the slogan "Down with corruption" is of an obviously extremist character because it calls for dismantling the existing political system in Russia and removing its current authorities.

Nevertheless, unless Russia tackles corruption, there will be no movement forward on reform. However, when then-President Putin's own precrisis fortune was put by one observer at over $40 billion in 2007, the chances of an anticorruption campaign having much impact are very low.[56] In fact, the trend in many ways seems to be in the other direction. According to a recent poll by the Levada Center, 60 percent of Russians believe that the scale of corruption at the top has grown over the past 10 years. Ten percent said corruption had gone down, while 23 percent felt that nothing had changed. In 2005, only 45 percent of respondents reported an increase in corruption.[57]

Other polling likewise suggests that corruption has gone from being the grease that makes the wheels of the Russian economy spin to a spreading sludge that slows them down. A recent online survey of over 10,000 businesspeople underscored the extent to which corruption is perceived as a systemic phenomenon that impedes modernization. Slightly over 23 percent of respondents pointed to corruption as a barrier to modernization, and 15.9 percent indicated that bureaucratic opposition was the problem. Only 9.5 percent pointed to Russia's dependence on world prices for raw materials and another 9.2 percent to Russia's lag in science and technology as the culprit. Not surprisingly, 68.7 percent were doubtful that Russia would hit its modernization marks by 2020, while only 16.4 percent were optimistic that the country would at least put in place the preconditions for realizing them.[58]

Yet other accounts reinforce the enormity of the problem. UBS/Campden Research recently polled 25 businessmen whose businesses did at least $100 million in annual volume, and who had a minimum personal worth of $50 million (half of the respondents' worth was $100 million to $500 million). The poll found that 84 percent kept their money overseas—with Cyprus, Switzerland, and the Virgin Islands the most popular—not for the tax breaks, but rather to keep it safe. (Net capital flight from Russia was likely to reach $22 billion in 2010.[59]) Across the board, the respondents complained of corruption and bureaucracy, especially in the regions. Because of the economy's history of unpredictability, they claimed not to plan further out than 2 years. The only thing they felt certain about was an unfriendly business climate. All but two were ready to sell out for a good price; just under half were ready to do this in the next 2 to 4 years. Only a third hoped to pass on their businesses to their children; two-thirds said they would let their children decide for themselves what to do in life.[60]

Military Malaise

Russia faces still another major challenge to remaining a great power. Shortages of manpower and money have been relentlessly degrading the Russian military establishment since the collapse of the Soviet Union. During Soviet times, Russian scientific and technological innovation was focused on advancing the military-industrial sector. When that sector crumbled, so did Russia's high-tech sector, aggravating the challenges Russia now faces to revive its military.[61]

The Russian-Georgian war in August 2008 gave some the illusion of a well-run military machine. Russian forces fought well relative to those of Georgia, demonstrating impressive surge capability and mobility and achieving swift victory. However, a Russian commander at one point had to borrow a satellite phone from a journalist to communicate with his forces, the Russian army relied on old compasses and maps instead of modern satellite-based systems to orient itself, and Georgian troops shot down a Russian strategic bomber that was employed for aerial reconnaissance instead of an unmanned aerial vehicle (UAV). Russia's shortcomings in the war gave additional, real-life ammunition to advocates of the long-anticipated and still controversial military reform, reorganization, and rearmament programs now under way.[62]

Demographic constraints on military manpower are already noticeable. By 2016, it is estimated that the number of young men of draft age will be half that of two decades earlier.[63] Sergei Stepashin, a former prime minister and now head of Russia's federal audit chamber, warned in 2007 that the "reduction in the size of the population and the reduction of population density . . . will create the danger of weakening Russia's political, economic, and military influence in the world."[64]

The pool of 18-year-old men available for drafting into 12-month tours of duty can no longer support a one-million-man army. From 2008 to 2017, this pool of prospective recruits will shrink by almost two-fifths, from 1.021 million to 626,000. Moreover, in 2006, of the 20 regions in the Russian Federation where births exceeded deaths, 19 were "republics" or "autonomous districts" for non-Russian peoples. Of these, the only two with natural increases of over 1 percent were Ingushetiya and Chechnya, where the net increase was almost 2 percent.[65] The higher birth rates among Russia's historically Muslim communities mean increasing numbers of draftees will hail from these areas. This trend is likely to present growing challenges for commanders. In July 2010, a fight between Dagestani and Russian soldiers broke out in one Moscow division. The fracas involved more than 200 soldiers, and a video of the melee wound up being posted on YouTube.[66]

Last summer, after Medvedev called for an overhaul of the draft system, Vasily Smirnov, deputy head of the General Staff, floated several possible measures to increase the size of the draft pool and to fight widespread draft evasion. Student deferments would be dramatically reduced, and men would be available until age 30 for the draft, up from 27. Rather than being summoned, 18-year-olds would have to show up on their own at local draft boards for registration and case dispensation. Without a proper document from their draft board, young men would not be able to travel abroad. These measures provoked instant criticism. Abandonment of student deferments, it was argued, would further degrade the professional preparation of Russia's young male population for civilian employment. Requirement of draft board certificates for travel abroad would simply enlarge the category of officials to whom bribes would be paid to dodge the draft. No longer would it be just doctors and draft board members getting money under the table, but also police, border officials, and military police.[67]

The Russian military budget stood at $61 billion in 2009, compared to $663.3 billion for the United States, $98.8 billion for China, $69.3 billion for Britain, and $67.3 for France.[68] That budget was set last summer to increase from 2.6 percent of the national budget in 2010 to 3.2 percent in 2013, but is now being revised upward to around 3.5 to 4 percent of GDP.[69] Even at the higher rate, however, Russia's spending on its military establishment will still lag far behind that of the United States and even China, and be closer to the amount spent by Britain and France. In comparison to China, the real gap will probably be even wider, given the corruption that some Russians claim eats away at 30 to 50 percent of Russian spending on new weapons and Russian estimates that China's real military budget is 30 to 40 percent greater than its declared budget.[70]

Defense Minister Anatoly Serdyukov has admitted that he was, "quite frankly, dismayed by the volumes of stealing" that he found when he arrived at the ministry. The basic budget problems are exacerbated by the fact that Russia spent almost nothing on rearming the military from 1991 to 2000. Much of the military's equipment and weapons systems are outdated, obsolete, or nonfunctioning, so Russia is playing serious catch-up vis-à-vis both the United States and China. Most serious military analysts conclude that Russia will have to choose sectors in which to invest, rather than maintain a globally capable force. Serdyukov has pointed to the "nuclear deterrence forces, the space forces, air defense, aviation, communications" as the priorities in the new rearmament program.[71]

The ability to project military power over long distances is a critical difference between a superpower and a great power. Russia, however, will not be able to project sizable conventional forces far beyond its borders consistently and repeatedly for many years to come. After Russia's armed action against Somali pirates in the Gulf of Aden in May 2010, General Nikolai Makarov, head of the General Staff, said that Russia did not plan to send more warships to the gulf because of financial problems. (This decision has since been reversed.[72]) However, there was no cause for worry, Makarov said, since North Atlantic Treaty Organization (NATO) and EU naval force ships were always on duty in the gulf, and "we maintain cooperation with them, hold exercises as well as exchange information."[73]

A few weeks later, Minister Serdyukov reportedly told a closed session of the Federation Council that creating new military bases abroad "is an expensive treat; we already have four military bases outside Russia. Raising their number further would probably be too burdensome." Referring to the loss of the Soviet-era naval base in the Gulf of Aden, Serdyukov reportedly said, "Of course, it would have suited us to have a base there, where our ships could refuel, but objectively we must proceed from the state's financial capabilities."[74] In fall 2010, the Foreign Ministry denied that Russia intended to hold talks with Vietnam on restoring its naval base at Cam Ranh Bay.[75]

Russia's state plan will now call for spending $613 billion on new arms between 2011 and 2020, according to Serdyukov.[76] This is up from the approximately $420.7 billion called for in a previous draft plan that provoked criticism for shortchanging the military's real needs. Lieutenant-General Oleg Frolov, for example, the acting chief of acquisitions for the armed forces, argued that the earlier amount would only cover the needs of strategic nuclear forces, air defense, and the air force. To meet the additional requirements for rearming ground troops, navy, and space forces, Frolov maintained, almost three times as much would be necessary: some $1.1 trillion instead of the proposed $420.7 billion.[77] While the additional moneys will help to rearm Russia, they will put a tremendous and probably unsustainable strain on Russia's budget down the line while still falling short of the sums that Frolov insisted are actually needed.[78]

While it is not surprising that a Ministry of Defense official would lobby for more funds, Russia in fact will need to spend much more than it envisioned if it is to have a first-rate military in the decades ahead. Already, Russia's strategic strength lies in missiles and nuclear warheads left over from the Soviet era. In other areas, for example, Russia's Pacific Fleet strategic submarines will need to be decommissioned in the next 2 to 3 years, and the Northern Fleet will face the same situation 7 to 10 years from now, according to analyst Igor Korotchenko.[79] On air defenses, Russian Air Force generals claim that Russia lags behind its "virtual adversary" by 20 to 30 years and is not capable of repelling every threat even from North Korea and Iran.[80] Ground forces are undergoing radical reorganization under Russia's ongoing military reform but still make do without modern weapons and global positioning systems or UAV support and still rely on analog rather than digital communications.[81]

However, Russia's own defense industry sector is atrophying while continuing to hang on largely on the remaining but dissipating momentum from the Soviet era. The average age of employees in the sector is around 55, and three-quarters of its equipment is worn out.[82] Rather than reviving the sector, Russia is increasingly going abroad to shop for the latest in military technology. The most prominent recent examples include the purchase of Mistral amphibious assault ships from France, UAVs from Israel, armored personnel carriers from Italy, and even digital receivers for its Global Navigation Satellite Systems from India.[83] According to some Russian forecasts, Russia may spend as much as $12 billion in the next 5 years to buy defense technologies from European and Israeli companies.[84] After meeting with Defense Secretary Robert M. Gates in September, Serdyukov announced that his ministry would quickly put together a list of specific products and technologies that it would be interested in acquiring from the United States.[85]

Commenting on the decision to buy UAVs from Israel, Air Force Commander Colonel-General Alexander Zelin conceded that "we would be happy to buy our own devices, but unfortunately they don't meet the high standards that this kind of weapons is supposed to meet."[86] One analyst concluded, "The VPK [military-industrial complex] is losing the capability of putting out arms." In the words of Aleksandr Khramchikhin, "We are becoming dependent on imports in an ever greater number of directions, and no one hides this. We will be able to purchase weapons only in the West, because only there are they modern."[87] Even as the Russian military begins to buy more foreign-made equipment, it likely will not be able to afford enough to keep up with the geopolitical standards and tasks the political leadership will inevitably want to set for them.

The "Near Abroad"

As hard as Russia has been rocked by the global financial crisis, undermined by demographic decline, and sapped by corruption, poor governance, and military decay, many of the other former Soviet republics have been hit even harder. While energy-rich Kazakhstan and Azerbaijan still wield substantial economic power, vast numbers of unemployed from Ukraine to Tajikistan seek work in Russia and send remittances to support their families back home. Ukraine and Belarus share Russia's trend toward population decline and are still vulnerable to Russian pressure tactics on energy supplies.[88] As a result, Russia arguably still has as much influence across Eurasia today as it did in the 1990s. This influence, however, is not automatic, varies on a case-by-case basis, and often backfires. Moreover, it will probably decline in the decades ahead as the former Soviet states ramp up their engagement with states around them and beyond.

Russia enjoys many soft power plusses in the former Soviet near abroad. Russian private investment in telecoms and other sectors has been substantial and successful but relatively non-political.[89] The reach and popularity of Russian television are vast but not necessarily decisive to the outcome of political contests. Soft power, and even hard power, does not necessarily produce pliable partners. Having dealt with their powerful Russian neighbor for centuries, the former Soviet states are experienced at saying the right things to please Moscow while pursuing their own national interests.

Russia's close neighbors are all also adept at courting outside international ties to counter-balance Russian influence, and the greater Moscow's influence, the greater the perceived need to engage other outside partners. The United States and the EU have vastly increased their presence throughout the near abroad in recent years. Since the collapse of the Soviet Union, the United States has been the countervailing power of choice, but European states, Turkey, and even Iran have also offered options along the way.

Now, rich and booming China has finally emerged as a substantial addition to this mix, with the opening of a major gas pipeline from Turkmenistan in late 2009 and investments and loans across the region.[90] After years of trying not to attract attention, China suddenly looms as a much greater player across Central Asia and even into the Caucasus and Ukraine and other Western states.[91] Turkmenistan, meanwhile, is pushing ahead to diversify its energy export ties with not only China but also Western companies, giving short shrift to Russia, its traditional partner.[92]

In Ukraine, Russian state-sponsored media interference backfired and contributed to the Orange Revolution in 2004. Russia was better served by a more subtle approach in 2010, after which Moscow used the promise of cheaper gas prices to gain an extension of its lease on the base in Sevastopol for the Russian Black Sea fleet. However, while the new Viktor Yanukovych administration in Kyiv has moved quickly to reprioritize relations with Moscow, it is not a Russian patsy. Yanukovych and his supporters have their own economic agenda and constituents that must be protected.[93] In Kyrgyzstan, a Russian media campaign arguably played a role in President Kurmanbek Bakiyev's ouster last April. But Russia declined to intervene militarily to staunch the subsequent bloodshed then and in June, in contrast to 1990, when elite Soviet troops were deployed to the region after similar violence.[94] Medvedev subsequently signed a statement of cooperation on Kyrgyzstan when he met with President Obama in Washington on June 24.

Even more recently, after a natural gas pricing dispute erupted in June 2010, Moscow is now aiming its media guns at President Alyaksandar Lukashenka in Belarus. However, the Russian campaign has arguably had little effect except to motivate Lukashenka to court Georgian leader Mikheil Saakashvili, downgrade the effort to seek some sort of union with Russia, and call for lessening dependence on Russia and for establishing new markets and sources of investment.[95] Although a Russian-led Customs Union with Kazakhstan and Belarus came into force on July 1, 2010, the widening dispute with Belarus, nationalist opposition in Kazakhstan, and Russia's unilateral ban on grain exports have underscored its fragility and cast doubt on its future viability.[96]

Russia was quick to employ hard power against Georgia in August 2008, but Georgia may be the only former Soviet state where this could have happened: bordering Russia, with a tiny army and population, and with rebellious and ethnically diverse regions that have historically looked to Russia for support against Tbilisi. Russia was reluctant to intervene militarily in the Tajik civil war in 1992,[97] and has not done so 18 years later in Kyrgyzstan. The argument could be made that Russia would be forced to intervene in Kazakhstan, not in the context of political disagreements with Astana, but should there be a total collapse of state power across the country with no signs of quick restitution. Russia's long border with Kazakhstan, the still-large ethnic Russian population in that country, and Russia's sizable investments in Kazakhstan's economy might indeed bring that about and might even enjoy the support of many Kazakhs, the majority of whom still view Russia favorably.

Still, while Russia is currently in the throes of reorganizing its conventional forces, the jury will be out for quite some time on whether the "new look" will give Russia a more effective tool for projecting military power beyond its borders. Meanwhile, the usefulness of the Russian-led Collective Security Treaty Organization (CSTO) Rapid Reaction Force is questionable, an impression reinforced by the failure of the CSTO to deploy it last year to Kyrgyzstan or to provide Kyrgyzstan with any military aid at all.

While Russia successfully concluded the war with Georgia and the Russian military remains entrenched on internationally recognized Georgian territory, Russia has not necessarily won the peace. Others in the Commonwealth of Independent States were reminded of the worst aspects of having an overbearing Russian neighbor and stimulated to reinforce and seek out ties with other regional powers.[98] Whatever their discomfort with Georgian President Saakashvili, none has recognized the independence of South Ossetia or Abkhazia, and all have been supported in this nonrecognition and nose-thumbing at Russia by China.[99]

China

Despite the disagreement over recognition of South Ossetia and Abkhazia, Sino-Russian official relations for now are arguably the best since the 1969 border clashes.[100] Russia is working hard to smooth relations with China, and China is wary of feeding any Russian concerns over the future. When Chinese President Hu Jintao visited Moscow to help celebrate the 65th anniversary of Victory in Europe Day, he and Medvedev stressed the importance of the "strategic partnership" between China and Russia.[101] In Khabarovsk in the Far East 2 months later, Foreign Minister Lavrov underscored that the region's two biggest countries, China and India, were both "strategic partners" of Russia, and that it was important that both look on Russia as a "comfortable partner."[102] In September, meeting with the Valdai discussion group, Putin accused foreign experts of "always trying to frighten [Russia] about China," which he denied presented a current or future threat.[103] Several weeks later in Beijing, Medvedev said that relations with China were now "at their highest point."[104]

Nevertheless, the sharp reversal in Russia and China's relative standing in the world is "the starkest in a short period during peacetime for any two neighboring great powers in modern history."[105] Chinese analysts already view China, the United States, and the EU as the world's dominant political-economic powers, with China having surpassed Russia.[106] According to one Russian expert, these Chinese analysts include Russia in the second tier of world powers at best, along with Japan and India, but sometimes even below this. In any case, according to this same expert, China and the United States are already the most important world powers.[107] When Medvedev, during his recent summit in Beijing, fired Moscow mayor Yuri Luzhkov, it quickly gave rise to the joke among Russians that everything is made in China, even the decree dismissing Luzhkov.

At the same time, Russia's relations with the West are in flux. Traditional Russian paranoia about the intentions of NATO and the United States is currently abating. After the Soviet collapse, Russian mistrust had begun to grow when the first prospects for NATO enlargement appeared in spring 1993, and surged particularly after the March 1999 bombing of Serbia. At their summit in Moscow in May 2002, however, in the wake of 9/11, Presidents George W. Bush and Putin issued a joint declaration on the "new strategic relationship" between Russia and

America, signed the Moscow Treaty on nuclear reductions, and endorsed the NATO–Russia Council (NRC) created a few days earlier by the NATO summit in Rome.

That high point of Russian-American relations under Bush-Putin began to fray after the invasion of Iraq in May 2003. Five years later, the NRC went into eclipse after Russia fought with Georgia, stationed troops in Abkhazia and South Ossetia, and recognized their independence. In 2009, however, the pendulum began to move in the other direction. In the wake of President Obama's invitation to reset and Medvedev's call for "modernization" and closer contacts with the West, Washington and Moscow negotiated the new Strategic Arms Reduction Treaty (New START) and Moscow agreed to the transit across Russia of U.S. and NATO supplies for forces fighting in Afghanistan. By November 2010, Putin's successor joined in reviving the NRC when he attended the NATO summit in Lisbon, where he agreed that Russia would cooperate on theater missile defenses with NATO and even explore participation in a broader U.S.-planned Europe-wide network.[108]

While most Russians are nevertheless probably still focused on the West and NATO as a potential threat, it is possible to detect signs that they are beginning to be really spooked by China's dramatic rise in the world and the implications for relations between the two countries in the decades ahead. Since Russia and China began to rebuild ties in 1989, for example, arms sales have been a key part of the self-described "strategic relationship." Sales and coproduction deals played an important role in building China's military capabilities, particularly in aircraft. But this facet of the relationship is now beset by tensions in the wake of China's 2004 decision to break its 1996 coproduction deal with Russia on a variant of the Su-27 fighter, which China attempted to reverse-engineer and produce as the J–11. China has not been able to duplicate the engine for the J–11 and still relies on Russia for advanced jet engines. Nevertheless, China's violation of the contract and increasing rivalry with Russia as a source of weapons systems for third-country markets have understandably become impediments to technological sharing between the two countries.[109] Even in Central Asia, which Russians view as their backyard, China's pursuit of its own self-interest has begun to cut against Russian interests and reduced Russian leverage on Central Asian energy resources. China is a vast and courted market for Russian energy sales, but with the opening of the major gas pipeline from Turkmenistan to China in late 2009, China has broken Russia's monopoly on Central Asian energy.[110]

As a result of these and similar developments, one can already hear among close observers of the relationship the view that Russia now sees China as a major player that is bigger and more dynamic than Russia. In reality and in principle, some recently noted to this author, China already impinges on Russia's interests. As a pole in a multipolar world, China has grown so much that it presents a problem for Russia. According to this view, it is not quite to the point where Russia will side with the United States against China, because Russia does not want to turn China into an enemy. But if China threatens Russia, then Russia would look for allies.[111]

Russian and Chinese officials generally avoid portraying each other as a potential enemy, and indeed in the short term do everything they can to accentuate the positive. Russia and China have a program for joint economic cooperation to the year 2018 between Russia's Eastern Siberia and Far East regions and China's North-East provinces. Occasionally, however, candor brings forth a disquieting view of this regional cooperation. According to one analyst, the transportation infrastructure that will be built will just make it possible for China's "troops and military hardware . . . [to] get to the heart of Russia more quickly."[112] More generally, General Makarov, head of the General Staff, in July 2009 gave a presentation that some interpreted as clearly implying that NATO and China were "our most dangerous geopolitical adversaries." Several months later, Lieutenant-General Sergei Skokov, chief of staff of the Ground Forces, admitted that China was, in effect, "our potential enemy."[113]

On the Russian side, the greatest fear is the future of its thinly populated Far East. Dmitri Trenin, director of the Carnegie Endowment's Moscow Center, notes that "The fate of Russia will be decided east of the Urals, not west of the Urals."[114] Konstantin Kosachev, chairman of the Duma's International Affairs Committee, warns that if Russia does not "grow Siberia and the Far East, we'll remain on the sidelines" of international developments.[115] Medvedev this summer called the Far East's 25 percent decline in population since 1991 "unquestionably the most worrying and most dangerous trend in the district, and something that requires our constant attention." Lavrov argued that "there are no direct threats to Russia's national security here," although he conceded that "the potential for conflict does still exist in the region."[116]

Others put it far more strongly. They point to the great and increasing disparities between China and Russia, overall and across the Far East border. China's 1.32 billion population and $4.326 trillion GDP (in 2008), third largest in the world, dwarf Russia's 141 million people and $1.601 trillion economy, in ninth place globally. (In August 2010, China surpassed Japan to become the world's second-largest economy.)[117] The population density on the Chinese side of the Far East border is 62 times that on the Russian side.[118] Only 6 million Russians in the Far East and Eastern Siberia face 141 million Chinese in the two provinces across the border. Moreover, there is creeping "Chinification" on the Russian side of the border as increasing numbers of ethnic Chinese settle in the Far East and Eastern Siberia "under the slogan of strategic partnership."[119] The 2.8 million soldiers of China's People's Liberation Army outnumber Russia's one-million-member armed forces.[120] In just the two military districts on the Chinese side of the border—Shenyang and Beijing—Chinese forces are stronger than all of Russia's conventional armed forces from Kaliningrad in Europe to Kamchatka in the Far East.[121]

Analysts in Moscow do not foresee a conflict with China across the Far Eastern border for at least 20 years, if then.[122] Nevertheless, both sides have already begun to hedge their bets. China held a major military exercise across the border from the Russian Far East in 2009, and Russia's "Vostok-2010," its largest exercise since the collapse of the Soviet Union, focused on the Far East in mid-2010.[123] While Russian officialdom and official press refrained from commenting on the point, one Russian analyst pointed out that the Chinese exercise was clearly a "rehearsal of aggression against Russia."[124]

Indeed, the views of some Russian analysts verge on the apocalyptic. China is preparing for war, according to Aleksandr Aladdin, and could start Russia's collapse by sabotaging Russian infrastructure as far away as the Urals and central Russia. China will try to expand into Russia's Far East peacefully, predicts Aleksandr Khramchikhin, but he does not rule out the use of force. The spark could be a domestic crisis that causes Chinese leaders to seize Russian territory in the Far East in order to distract the Chinese population from civil war. Otherwise, for the next several decades, China will focus on resolving the Taiwan issue. After that, China will seriously take on Russia.[125]

"Vostok-2010" concluded with a limited, "low-yield" nuclear strike against the notional opponent, described as a large separatist bandit force.[126] Analysts pointed out that the bandit scenario was absurd and that Russia's forces were clearly rehearsing how to fight a full-fledged war against regular army groupings and armored vehicles.[127] They also pointed out that a Russian nuclear strike would only invite a Chinese nuclear response. In their view, the only way to deter China from starting a war in the Far East would be for Russia to field credible and impressive conventional forces.[128]

The report card on "Vostok-2010" is still incomplete, as is an assessment of how far the "new look" to be achieved by Russia's military reform has moved beyond an aspirational plan.[129] Nevertheless, comparisons of the previous year's Russian "Zapad-2009" with Chinese exercises were not favorable. Russia's crack Taman combined arms brigade reportedly took 7 days to travel the 900 kilometers to the exercise range, while Chinese regiments were said routinely to take only 5 days to traverse analogous 2,400-kilometer spans.[130] The least that could be said about "Vostok-2010," according to one observer, was that it signaled to China that Russia was not yet prepared simply to surrender.[131] Another expert, however, has judged that it demonstrated progress in achieving the goal of major structural reform of the Russian military.[132]

In the meantime, Russia is doing everything possible to keep China close to it diplomatically, while also using reset to draw closer to the United States. Since the end of the Cold War, China and Russia have cooperated strategically to resist U.S. power. Even here, however, there have been limits to Russian-Chinese cooperation, as both have regarded their separate relationships with the United States as more important than their ties to each other. Nevertheless, American power has pushed Russia and China together and they have worked together in various ways to try to constrain the United States. Their shared view of the United States as too powerful, irresponsible, and bent on achieving hegemony and dominance was one of many factors that contributed to the Russian-Chinese arms relationship described above.

The Brazil, Russia, India, China (BRIC) grouping is one of the more recent manifestations of Russian and Chinese efforts to cooperate to constrain U.S. power. Bringing together Russia and China with India and Brazil, the BRIC was actually first conceived in 2001 by Goldman Sachs investment bankers as an investment strategy focused on the four rising economic powerhouses. The four countries then adopted the concept and sought to transform it into another venue through which to restructure global economic relations, in particular America's impact on global markets in the wake of the global financial crisis, and Russia hosted the first summit of BRIC presidents in Ekaterinburg in June 2009.[133]

When Russia is worried about a stronger, more assertive United States, its BRIC ties are more pronounced. When this is not the case, Russian worries about China come more to the fore. At the same time, Russia also worries about U.S. ties with China eclipsing its ties with Russia. All are elements of Russian policy, and all have been manifest in recent years. In early 2010, with Russia increasingly concerned about China both in the Russian Far East and in Central Asia, both as an economic actor and a military threat, Foreign Minister Lavrov underscored the need to track "China's increasing role in international affairs, including from the angle of the consequences of Beijing's activity for our global and regional interests."

But the Russian foreign minister drew attention to the "fundamental importance of anchoring China to positions of acting jointly with us," and fretted about perceived U.S. efforts to marginalize formats such as the BRIC and the Shanghai Cooperation Organization that bring together Russia and China but do not include the United States.[134] Russia seems to be worried that Washington could partner with China and leave Russia in the ditch, isolated or ignored. U.S. trade with China, after all, stood at $366 billion in 2009, compared to just $24 billion with Russia.[135]

Iran

After the Iranian-supported Hizballah frustrated the Israeli army in Lebanon in 2006, Yevgeny Satanovsky, head of the Near East Institute in Moscow, warned that President Mahmoud Ahmadinejad was "testing the region's strength" and would have nuclear weapons in "two or three years' time."[136] According to Satanovsky, who represents a school of thought in Moscow, "the Shiite crescent, from Lebanon and Syria to the south of Iraq, Saudi Arabia's eastern province, and the minor monarchies of the Persian Gulf, are a priority zone of interest." Iran's "nuclear programs and, in the very near future, nuclear weapons are a guarantee of its inviolability." Satanovsky speculated that after settling matters with its Persian Gulf rivals, Iran would turn its sights to its former "northern territories" in the Caucasus and Central Asia. By 2050, Satanovsky predicted, Russia's population would shrink to 100 million while Iran's—now over 70 million—would grow by 20 million, and Iran would "be fully organized in terms of oil, gas, and nuclear technologies."[137]

Less than 3 years later, one of the first public signs that Moscow was considering toughening its stance toward Tehran and moving closer to Washington concerned the S–300 long-range air defense missile system. Even before Obama's swearing in as President, hints began that Moscow was rethinking the deal and perhaps moving toward holding up the transfer of the missiles to Iran.[138] By February 4, 2009, Rosoboroneksport General Director Anatoly Isaykin stated publicly that the S–300 contract still needed presidential approval for the system's transfer to Iran to be executed.[139]

However, Putin and Lavrov in September 2009 reportedly regarded Iran as a rising power in the Middle East and were therefore disinclined to confront it directly.[140] This was still the perception among analysts in Moscow in May 2010. Iran was likely to become the regional power of the "first rank" in the Middle East and Persian Gulf, so Russia could not afford to ignore or anger it. With a population of 73.6 million, Iran already determined stability in the region. One expert called for a "cautious partnership" and argued that Russia's approach to Iran needed to be "cooperation and deterrence" everywhere.[141]

Around that time, however, as negotiations quickened on the final language of UN Security Council Resolution 1929, which would pass with Russian support in June, Putin and Medvedev had already begun to push the envelope of Russian commentary critical of Iran, and Ahmadinejad in return insulted both. After passage of the sanctions measure, Medvedev's treatment of Iran in his July 12 speech to Russia's ambassadors abandoned any diplomatic pretenses designed to give Russia, and Iran, wiggle room. "It is obvious that Iran is coming close to the possession of potential that could in principle be used to create nuclear weapons," the Russian president stated. This was against the background of Medvedev's call, in the same speech, for a "paradigm shift" in Russian foreign policy and "special modernization alliances with our main international partners. . . . First and foremost with countries like Germany, France, Italy, the EU as a whole, the United States of America."[142] Ahmadinejad responded by calling Medvedev's remarks "an advertisement of a propaganda show, which is going to be performed by America." "Why does the Russian president want to have a role in this play?" asked the Iranian president. "We are sorry to see this. They should not be deceived."[143]

Both sides subsequently tried to use the late August ceremony marking the launch of preparations to load fuel at the Bushehr nuclear power station, some 10 years late, to cool off the rhetoric. Nevertheless, Russian suspicion of Iran's nuclear program and regional ambitions remained high, as did Russian incentives to work more closely with the United States against the common threat. The tough decree that Medvedev issued on September 22 spelling out Russian sanctions of Iran pursuant to UN Security Council Resolution 1929, including nontransfer of the S–300 system, was a clear signal to Tehran intended to reinforce the point.[144]

Implications for the United States

In the coming decades, Russia will retain its status as a nuclear power and its hold on one of the UN Security Council's five veto-wielding seats. On other measures of its status as a great power, however, Russia is likely to slip further behind relative to today's great and rising powers, especially the United States and China. Based on current high world commodity prices, especially oil, Russia's newfound affluence will remain vulnerable to market fluctuations and to the possible rise of alternative energy sources. Russia's wealth will also decline in relative terms should it fail to invest today's easy profits in the industries and knowledge sectors essential for prospering in an ever more technologically challenging future. Russia's economy, mired in corruption and deteriorating demographics, conceivably may not even be able to sustain today's Moscow-centric growth in prosperity.

Russia's conventional armed forces will not be able to project substantial and sustained power far beyond Russian borders. They will still overshadow the military establishments of Russia's surrounding former Soviet neighbors, and therefore retain some leverage. But the multiple challenges to Moscow of a military intervention into any of these states will dictate extreme caution and consequent reluctance to employ armed force. The exceptions may be in case of renewed tensions with Georgia or the wholesale collapse of the state in Kazakhstan.

Russia's greatest external challenge will be China. As the world's largest and fastest rising power, China already looms as a threat to Russia's hold on its sparsely populated Far East regions. Russia's increasingly weak position relative to China will raise the incentives for Russia not only to court Chinese good graces, but also to bolster its conventional military presence in the Far East as well as to retain tactical nuclear weapons as a deterrent of last resort in both the Far East and in Russia's European western regions. At the same time, Russia's concerns may lead Moscow to cooperate more consistently with the United States and Europe, both directly and in the Asia-Pacific region, as economic and military counterweights to rising Chinese power.

Trenin has written that "a key challenge for Russia's foreign policy will be to learn to live alongside a China that is strong, dynamic, assertive, and increasingly advanced."[145] According to Trenin, Russia is absolutely committed to stable and peaceful relations with China but is also wary: the current Chinese Communist Party leadership could eventually be replaced by more nationalistic elements; China could also become embroiled in domestic problems.[146] Already, China's increasing confidence and assertiveness are casting a "longer and thicker" shadow over Russia. Together with the global financial crisis, the Russian-Georgian war, and the new Obama administration, a rising China contributed to the reset of relations between Washington and Moscow. Russia's "backwardness" relative to the West and even to some emerging powers dictated a modernization drive, in Trenin's view, which in turn required improved relations with the United States and the West.[147]

Fedor Lukyanov, editor of *Russia in Global Affairs*, similarly views China's growth as becoming the dominant factor in Russian foreign policy and forcing its reorientation, primarily toward the United States. The current high level of Russian-Chinese relations "does not save [them] from complications in the future." Russia needs a "sustainable presence" in the Asia-Pacific region, but its "central problem" today is avoiding becoming China's "satellite." In general, Lukyanov writes, "Russia cannot afford to have bad relations with China, as this may bring very big risks in all areas. . . . At the same time, a search for a soft system of counterweights will probably become the leitmotif of Russia's policy in Asia and beyond."[148]

Russia and the United States share the problem of how to deal with a China on the rise, but from different angles, according to Lukyanov. Russian perceptions of the U.S. military presence in Asia are very different from those of its presence on Russia's western and southern borders. Cooperation in the Asia-Pacific region, therefore, might become a new basis for U.S.-Russian relations once reset achieves all its aims. Washington and Moscow will need a new agenda, and its centerpiece could be the Asia-Pacific region after New START is ratified and the arms control track comes to an end.[149]

Similarly, Sergei Karaganov, head of Russia's Council on Foreign and Defense Policy, warned in February 2010 of the danger of a "sagging" Russia "sliding past the status of a 're-spected younger brother' and turning into an outright raw and energy appendage of Great China." Avoiding this fate, according to Karaganov, demands that Moscow continue to work for "rapprochement" with Washington, including joint efforts, along with Asian countries, to develop Siberia and the Russian Far East.[150] In September 2010, Karaganov proposed the United States and Russia play "an important role" in the rapid creation of a security system in East and South Asia, not to deter China militarily according to "old methods" but to fill what he called the security "vacuum" forming around an "increasingly powerful China." He also urged the creation of a security system in and around the Persian Gulf, with security guarantees that at this point could only be offered by Russia and the United States, presumably working together.[151]

A rising and potentially threatening Iran may also be spurring Russia to move closer to U.S. positions because of Russia's own security concerns, and not simply to butter up Washington. Analysts in Moscow are already focusing on how to deter a nuclear Iran and prevent it from becoming a regional bully. One analyst recently suggested that the ultimate future counter to a nuclear Iran may have to be Article Five–type guarantees to Iran's threatened neighbors, including Israel and Saudi Arabia, by the United States, Russia, and perhaps also China. This analyst saw a political strategic security alliance with the United States as the best outcome for Russia from the current reset process.[152]

Declining powers have rising vulnerabilities, but so do rising powers as they contest the established regional or global dominance of other major powers. The increasing weight and muscle flexing of a rising power may cause neighboring second-rank powers to move closer to the United States to counterbalance their increasingly assertive neighbor. This phenomenon extends beyond the Russian reaction to a rising China, arguably one of the several reasons for Moscow's "modernization" campaign and positive response to Washington's offer of reset. Across the Asia-Pacific rim, a number of China's neighbors have also moved closer to the United States as they have responded to a rising, increasingly assertive, and historically distrusted China.[153] Similarly, around the Persian Gulf and throughout the Middle East, many states look to the United States for security vis-à-vis a rising Iran even as they worry that the United States (or Israel) might try to solve the Iranian nuclear problem militarily.[154]

This opens up opportunities for sage diplomacy and leadership by the United States where American and Russian goals overlap. In fact, we may already be seeing the beginning of a shift toward a new triangulation paradigm, particularly when it comes to China. Several years ago, before the global financial crisis hit, Bobo Lo speculated that Russia, reacting to "strategic tension" with China down the road, could "gravitate slowly back to Europe and become part of a larger Western consensus."[155] China's continued spectacular growth and Russia's postcrisis slowdown may have dramatically accelerated that development by many years.

It is therefore likely that long-term concerns over the impact on Russian interests of a mighty China will encourage Moscow to seek common ground with Washington increasingly more often and more consistently, as was recently on display at the NATO–Russia Council summit in Lisbon. At the same time, China's fear of isolation and of Russian-American rapprochement may also encourage China to continue to treat the United States with a greater degree of caution than contestation. This appeared to be the case when China, rather than striking out on its own, in the end voted for the most recent Iran sanctions resolution in the UN Security Council.[156] A continuation of this dynamic could leave the United States in the catbird seat for many years to come.

Providing the United States continues to be a vibrant society and plays its hand well, it should have many strong cards to play as a worried Russia looks to reinforce its position against its rising and pressing Chinese neighbor. But Moscow's policy toward Washington is conditional on a U.S. approach that engages Russia in positive ways. If that policy were to change, it could push Russia and China closer together. This was what happened in some ways during the recent Bush administration as Moscow and Beijing cooperated to manage and constrain what they perceived as a strong and aggressive Washington. Since then, the Obama administration has worked hard to reset relations with Russia. On arms control and Iran, it has recognized Russia as an important power that can affect U.S. achievement of its policy aims. It has made clear that missile defense in Europe is not aimed at Russia. It has kept alive but not made a pressing priority of NATO membership for Georgia and Ukraine.

But this could change with a new administration in Washington, and if it does, it will affect Russian-Chinese relations. As much as Moscow has welcomed Washington's reset of relations, it has not managed to shake the worry that it is transitory. Foreign Minister Lavrov in early 2010 underscored what he described as attempts by "right-wing conservative forces" in the United States to force a reversal to the "confrontational policy of the previous administration."[157] Well before the midterm elections, Russian analysts echoed the same concern both publicly and privately.[158] Should such a U.S. policy reversal come to pass, Russia will find itself in a very uncomfortable world, stuck between a dominant United States and an assertive China, both of which impinge on Russia's perceived long-term interests. The United States, on the other hand, to the extent that it does not respect those interests, will not be able to make the most of the opportunity to derive significant benefits from Russia's concerns about China and to work with Russia to face the challenges that China will increasingly present to both countries.

Notes

[1] "Putin's Keynote Speech to State Council—Text," Rossiya TV, February 8, 2008, CEP20080208950541 (Open Source Center product number).

[2] Anders Aslund and Andrew Kuchins, *The Russia Balance Sheet* (Washington, DC: Peterson Institute for International Economics, Center for Strategic and International Studies, April 2009), 42–43. Throughout this paper, the author has not attempted to sort out whether a particular observer has used gross domestic product figures based on nominal values or adjusted for purchasing power parity, or whether the source has used International Monetary Fund, World Bank, or Central Intelligence Agency World Factbook figures.

[3] Ibid., 146; Anders Aslund, Sergei Guriev, and Andrew C. Kuchins, eds., *Russia After the Global Economic Crisis* (Washington, DC: Peterson Institute for International Economics, Center for Strategic and International Studies, and New Economic School, June 2010), 9.

[4] Poll by the All-Russia Center for the Study of Public Opinion. See Boris Tumanov, "Daydreaming at the Fence," Gazeta.ru, September 23, 2010, CEP20100923046011.

[5] Anastasiya Bashkatova, "Dokhody grazhdan pod bol'shim voprosom," *Nezavisimaya Gazeta*, November 15, 2010, available at <www.ng.ru/economics/2010-11-15/1_income.html>.

[6] Konstantin Smirnov, "Rossiyu nakrylo novoi volnoi krizisa. VVP padaet vtoroi mesyats nodryad," *Moskovskii Komsomolets*, September 24, 2010, available at <www.mk.ru/economics/articles/2010/09/23/531710-rossiyu-nakryilo-novoy-volnoy-krizisa.html>. For an analysis focusing on the fall in industrial production, see Anastasiya Bashtakova, "Novyi promyshlennyi spad nachalsya," *Nezavisimaya Gazeta*, September 30, 2010, available at <www.ng.ru/economics/2010-09-30/1_industry.html>.

[7] See especially Marshall I. Goldman, *Petrostate: Putin, Power, and the New Russia* (New York: Oxford University Press, 2008).

[8] Yegor T. Gaidar, *The Collapse of the Empire: Lessons for Modern Russia* (Washington, DC: Brookings Institution, 2007); Aslund and Kuchins, 59; and Aslund, Guriev, and Kuchins, 9–38, 259–260.

[9] Nicholas Eberstadt, *Russia's Peacetime Demographic Crisis: Dimensions, Causes, Implications* (Seattle: The National Bureau of Asian Research, NBR Project Report, May 2010), 293–294.

[10] Andrei Trenin and Dmitri Trenin, "The Wider Implications of the Russian-Armenian Defense Deal," RFE/RL, August 24, 2010, available at <www.rferl.org/content/The_Wider_Implications_Of_The_RussianArmenian_Defense_Deal/2136480.html>.

[11] Vladimir Mukhin, "Zhestokii schet Severnogo Kavkaza," *Nezavisimaya Gazeta*, June 11, 2010.

[12] Aleksandr Belov, head of the Movement against Illegal Immigration, on the "Matter of Principle" talk show, Center TV, September 29, 2010, CEP20101001950155.

[13] Eberstadt, 296, 298–299.

[14] "The Modernization of Russia's Foreign Policy. Q&A with Dmitri Trenin," Carnegie Endowment for International Peace, August 2, 2010, available at <http://carnegieendowment.org/publications/index.cfm?fa=view&id=41322>.

[15] United Nations Statistics Department, "National Accounts Main Aggregates Database," available at <http://unstats.un.org/unsd/snaama/resCountry.asp>. See also Eberstadt, 294, for slightly different percentages.

[16] Aslund and Kuchins, 19. Bovin was a regime insider and well-known commentator who would become post-Soviet Russia's first ambassador to Israel.

[17] Eberstadt, 26.

[18] Andrew E. Kramer, "In a Summer of Extremes, Russia's Response to Fires Does Little to Calm Anger," *The New York Times*, August 8, 2010; Michael Schwirtz, "Russian Fires Raise Fears of Radioactivity," *The New York Times*, August 11, 2010; and Sergei Turchenko and Anatoliy Dmitriyev, "S takoi vlast'yu my vse srogrim. Anomalnaya zhara postavila "dvoyku" rossiiskoi gosudarstvennoi sisteme," *Svobodnaya Pressa*, August 13, 2010, available at <www.svpressa.ru/society/article/28988/>.

[19] Eberstadt, 26, 192–193.

[20] For a thorough survey, see the interview with ethnographer Viktor Nikolayev, a former deputy in the Leningrad Soviet, in "Rossiya-2010: v ozhidaniii raspada," *Svobodnaya Pressa*, June 10, 2010, available at <www.svpressa.ru/society/article/26211/>.

[21] Aslund, Guriev, and Kuchins, 10, 12.

[22] Author's observations, May 2010.

[23] "Zachem vam kompyuter?" Press-vypusk No. 1549, available at <http://wciom.ru/novosti/press-vypusk/press-vypusk/single/13710.html>.

[24] Aslund, Guriev, and Kuchins, 14.

[25] Aslund and Kuchins, 44–45.

[26] John W. Parker, *Persian Dreams: Moscow and Tehran Since the Fall of the Shah* (Washington, DC: Potomac Books, 2009), 130–131, 166–167, 354, fn. 128; and Joe Nocera, "Unyielding, An Oligarch vs. Putin," *The New York Times*, November 6, 2010.

[27] Aslund and Kuchins, 52, 60–61.

[28] Ibid., 47, 69; Aslund, Guriev, and Kuchins, 13.

[29] Aslund and Kuchins, 146; Aslund, Guriev, and Kuchins, 9, 24–25.

[30] Aslund and Kuchins, 147; Aslund, Guriev, and Kuchins, 9–10, 24–25, 257.

[31] "Putin's Keynote Speech to State Council—Text"; "Medvedev 12 November State-of-the-Nation Address to Russian Parliament—Full Text," November 13, 2009, CEP20091113950187.

[32] Sergei Guriev and Oleg Tsyvinsky, "Ratio economica: Vot on kakoi, zastoy," *Vedomosti*, June 22, 2010.

[33] Personal communication with the author, June 2010.

[34] "Medvedev Speech to Envoys Notes 'Paradigm Shift in International Relations,'" Russian Federation President Web site, July 12, 2010, CEP20100713009001.

[35] Igor Yurgens et al., "Russia in the 21st Century: Vision for the Future," January 2010, available at <www.riocenter.ru/files/INSOR%20Russia%20in%20the%2021st%20century_ENG.pdf>.

[36] Aleksandra Samarina, "Povestka dnya dlya presidenta—2012. InSoR: Medvedev vedyet 'tikhuyu voynu,'" available at <www.ng.ru/politics/2010-08-05/1_povestka.html>.

[37] Charles Grant, "Observations from Russia," *Insight*, Centre for European Reform, September 23, 2010.

[38] Vladimir Milov, "Illyuziya krasivoy zhizni," *Gazeta*, September 27, 2010, available at <www.gazeta.ru/column/milov/4323088.shtml>.

[39] Eberstadt, 9–10, 12. Estimates are by the official Russian Federal State Statistical Service.

[40] Eberstadt, 282, 286, 288.

[41] Aslund and Kuchins, 91.

[42] Eberstadt, 30, 283–284.

[43] Eberstadt, 283–287.

[44] Anatoly Vishnevsky, "Hado delat' stavku na detey migrantov," *Novaya Gazeta*, October 22, 2010.

[45] Eberstadt, 30, 294.

[46] Aslund and Kuchins, 57.

[47] Katsuya Ito, "The Impact of Oil Price Volatility on Macroeconomic Activity in Russia," Economic Analysis Working Papers 9, no. 5, July 2010, available at <www.unagaliciamoderna.com/eawp/coldata/upload/impact_oil-price_volatility_russia.pdf>.

[48] Aslund and Kuchins, 59–60.

[49] "Sechin Says Gazprom Must Raise Game," *The Moscow Times Online*, June 21, 2010, CEP20100621964088.

[50] Eberstadt, 292–293.

[51] Aslund and Kuchins, 58.

[52] Medvedev meeting with "United Russia" activists, "Alternatives to Modernizing the Country Do Not Exist," May 28, 2010, available at <www.kremlin.ru/news/7885>.

[53] Aslund and Kuchins, 47–48, 51.

[54] Aleksandr Golts, "The Disarmaments Program," *Yezhednevnyy Zhurnal*, May 26, 2010, CEP20100526037004.

[55] Sergei Guriev, interview by Danila Galperovich at the June 2010 St. Petersburg International Economic Forum, in "Medvedev—ne Putin?" (Is Medvedev Putin?), Radio Liberty, June 19, 2010, available at <www.svobodanews.ru/articleprintview/2076719.html>.

[56] Stanislav Belkovsky, interview by Manfred Quiring, "One Should Not Overestimate Putin's Active Role," *Die Welt*, November 12, 2007, EUP20071112301004; Oleg Salmanov, "Money-Equidistant," *The New Times*, November 14, 2007, CEP20071116009011; and Luke Harding, "Putin, the Kremlin Power Struggle and the $40 bn Fortune," *The Guardian*, December 21, 2007, available at <www.guardian.co.uk/world/2007/dec/21/russia.topstories3/print>. Putin dismissed the reports as "just rubbish, excavated from someone's nose" and claimed his personal wealth consisted only of an apartment in St. Petersburg, two Soviet-era cars, a plot of land outside Moscow, and $149,000 in the bank (James Kilner, "Putin scoffs at rumours of huge wealth," Reuters, February 14, 2008, available at <http://uk.reuters.com/assets/print?aid=UKL1479180020080214>).

[57] "Most Russians note rise in corruption over past 10 years—poll," Interfax, July 21, 2010, CEP20100721950077.

[58] "Korruptsiya peresilit modernizatsiyu," *Yezhednevnaya Delovaya Gazeta*, October 1, 2010, available at <www.rbcdaily.ru/print.shtml?2010/10/01/focus/515069>.

[59] Yekaterina Mereninskaya, "Kapital ne uderzhalsya," Gazeta.ru, November 16, 2010, available at <www.gazeta.ru/financial/2010/11/16/3438036.shtml>.

[60] Olga Kuvshinova, "The Oligarch Is Modest," *Vedemosti*, May 28, 2010, available at <www.vedomosti.ru/newspaper/article/2010/05/28/235758>. In another survey, 40 percent of firms reported having to make frequent bribes; see Aslund, Guriev, and Kuchins, 32.

[61] Elina Bilevskaya, "Innovations to Protect Defense Capability," *Nezavisimaya Gazeta Online*, September 22, 2010, CEP20100923677005.

[62] Roger McDermott, "Russia's Conventional Armed Forces and the Georgian War," *Parameters* (Spring 2009), 65–80; Aleksandr Anatolyevich Khramchikhin, "Lessons of the 'Five-Day War': Did the Russian Army Change Following the 'Hot Date' of 08.08.08?" *Nezavisimoye Voyennoye Obozreniye Online*, August 13, 2010, CEP20100813358004.

[63] Aslund and Kuchins, 92.

[64] Eberstadt, 294–295.

[65] Ibid., 22.

[66] Georgii Trushin, "Za draku russkikh i dagestantsev otvetili ofitsery Kantemirovki," *Svobodnaya Pressa*, August 14, 2010, available at <www.svpressa.ru/accidents/article/29009/>. For a subsequent incident in Perm region, see Sergei Ishchenko, "'Islamskiy bunt' na aviabaze VVS pod Perm'yu," *Svobodnaya Pressa*, October 14, 2010, available at <http://svpressa.ru/society/article/32098/>.

[67] Vladimir Mukhin, "Den' 'X' dlya prizyvnikov," *Nezavisimaya gazeta*, August 4, 2010, available at <www.ng.ru/politics/2010-08-04/3_kartblansh.html>.

[68] "Rossiya predstoit za 10 let sozdat' 'novuyu armiyu'—bez sovremennogo oruzhiya reformy bessmyslenny," available at <www.newsru.com/russia/04aug2010/budget.html>. The figures are clearly those of SIPRI (see <http://en.wikipedia.org/wiki/List_of_countries_by_military_expenditures>). SIPRI's estimate of the Chinese defense budget falls far short of the $150 billion that the U.S. Defense Department has estimated as China's real budget, as opposed to its $70.3 billion published budget.

[69] Daniil Ayzenshtadt, "The Army Took a Stab at Trillions," Gazeta.ru, June 3, 2010, CEP20100607358003; Dmitry Gorenburg, "Russia's State Armaments Program 2020: Is the Third Time the Charm for Military Modernization?" available at <http://russiamil.wordpress.com/2010/10/12/russia%E2%80%99s-state-armaments-program-2020-is-the-third-time-the-charm-for-military-modernization/>; Viktor Myasnikov, "Russia Begins Renewal of Arms Race. Military Budget Sets Out for Growth at Record Pace," *Nezavisimoye Voyennoye Obozreniye Online*, October 25, 2010, CEP20101027037014.

[70] The corruption estimate is from Golts. The estimate of China's hidden defense expenditures is that of China expert Aleksandr Aladdin, who put China's declared 2010 defense budget at $78 billion, in Andrey Polunin, "China Is Expanding: First Taiwan, Then Siberia and the Far East—PRC is Building Roads Along Russo-Chinese Border at an Accelerated Pace," *Svobodnaya Pressa*, June 28, 2010, CEP20100629041016.

[71] Yuliya Taratuta, interview of Russian Defense Minister Anatoly Serdyukov, "'I Was Dismayed by Volumes of Stealing.' Defense Minister Anatoly Serdyukov Tells Newsweek Why Russia Should Spend Trillions on Arms, Why Defense Ministry Does Not Want to Buy Russian Ships, and How People Steal in Army," *Russkiy Newsweek Online*, October 4, 2010, CEP20101004037002.

[72] "Russian Navy's Anti-piracy Presence in Gulf of Aden to Continue in 2011," RIA-Novosti, November 3, 2010, CEP20101103950073.

[73] "Russia Does Not Plan to Send More Ships to Gulf of Aden," ITAR–TASS, May 7, 2010, CEP20100507950147.

[74] "Russia Can't Afford Opening New Bases Abroad, Says Defence Minister," ITAR–TASS, June 9, 2010, CEP20100609950129.

[75] "Russia Not Planning to Reopen Navy Base in Vietnam—Foreign Ministry," Interfax, October 29, 2010, CEP20101029950143.

[76] Ilya Arkhipov and Lyubov Pronina, "Russia Boosts Arms Spree to $613 Billion, Seeks U.S. Technology," Bloomberg.com, September 20, 2010.

[77] Ayzenshtadt.

[78] Sergei Aleksashenko, director of Macroeconomic Research at the Higher School of Economics in Moscow, estimates that military expenditures would explode to 29.4 percent of the federal budget in 2020 under current plans. Aleksashenko, presentation on "Russian Economy after the Global Crisis," Carnegie Endowment, Washington, DC, October 12, 2010.

[79] "Russian Pacific Fleet Strategic Subs Have 2–3 Years' Life Left in Them—Pundit," Center TV, June 2, 2010, CEP20100603950151.

[80] "General Says Russian Air Defenses in 'Complete Stagnation,'" newsru.com, May 13, 2010, CEP20100513037005.

[81] "Rossiya predstoit za 10 let sozdat' "novuyu armiyu"—bez sovremennogo oruzhiya reformy bessmyslenny," available at <www.newsru.com/russia/04aug2010/budget.html>.

[82] Aslund, Guriev, and Kuchins, 184; Eberstadt, 295–296.

[83] "Minoborony kupit bolshe 1,5 tysyach italyanskiykh bronevikov—russkiye "Tigry" okazalis ne nuzhniy," available at <www.newsru.com/russia/06aug2010/tigers_failed.html>; Golts.

[84] Ilya Arkhipov and Lyubov Pronina, "Russia Boosts Arms Spree to $613 Billion, Seeks U.S. Technology," Bloomberg News, Bloomberg.com, September 20, 2010.

[85] Taratuta interview.

[86] "Russian Domestic Industry Incapable of Building State-of-the-art UAVs," Interfax-AVN Online, August 16, 2010, CEP20100816950020.

[87] Aleksandr Khramchikhin in Yury Kotenok, "A Nanoarmy for a Nanocountry," Segodnya.ru, July 10, 2010, CEP20100712358035.

[88] Since the collapse of the Soviet Union, the population of Belarus has fallen by half a million and of Ukraine by almost 6 million. See Eberstadt, 20. On Russian energy pressure tactics, see Richard Andres and Michael Kofman, "European Energy Security: Potential Solutions for Reducing the Volatility of Ukraine-Russia Gas Pricing Disputes" (forthcoming).

[89] Aslund, Guriev, and Kuchins, 236, 239.

[90] "Turkmenistan-China Gas Pipeline Put in Operation," ITAR–TASS, December 14, 2009.

[91] Aslund, Guriev, and Kuchins, 238.

[92] Bruce Pannier, "Turkmenistan Tips Its Hand on Future Energy Exports," RFE/RL, August 22, 2010, available at <www.rferl.org/content/Turkmenistan_Tips_Its_Hand_On_Future_Energy_Exports/2134389.html>.

[93] "Ukraine Under Yanukovych: An Analytical Debate," Atlantic Council, August 23, 2010, available at <www.acus.org/event/ukraine-under-yanukovych-analytical-debate>.

[94] "The Pogroms in Kyrgyzstan. Executive Summary," International Crisis Group, Asia Report No. 193, August 23, 2010, EUP20100823167023.

[95] Michael Schwirtz, "In Information War, Documentary Is Latest Salvo," *The New York Times*, August 1, 2010; "Lukashenko Urges Lowering Dependence upon Russia," ITAR–TASS, June 25, 2010, CEP20100625950118.

[96] Farkhad Sharip, "Russia's Customs Union Tinged with Failure," *Asia Times Online*, August 20, 2010, available at <www.atimes.com/atimes/Central_Asia/LH20Ag01.html>.

[97] Parker, 57–81.

[98] Armenia even explored the possibility of rapprochement with Turkey but most recently has agreed to extend the lease on the Russian military base at Gyumri to the year 2044 ("FYI—Russian President Hails Significance of Remaining Military Base in Armenia," *Rossiya* 24, August 20, 2010, CEP20100820950152.

[99] See also the useful survey by Katinka Barysch, Centre for European Reform, "Who Is Winning Eastern Europe's Great Game?" *Insight*, July 19, 2010, available at <http://centreforeuropeanreform. blogspot.com/2010/07/who-is-winning-eastern-europes-great.html>.

[100] See Bobo Lo, *Axis of Convenience: Moscow, Beijing, and the New Geopolitics* (Washington, DC: Brookings Institution Press, 2008); and Richard Weitz, "Russian-Chinese Security Relations: Constant and Changing," in *The Russian Military Today and Tomorrow: Essays in Memory of Mary Fitzgerald*, ed. Stephen J. Blank and Richard Weitz (Carlisle, PA: U.S. Army War College, Strategic Studies Institute, 2010), 389–453.

[101] "Russia, China to Continue Strategic Partnership Course," Interfax, May 9, 2010, CEP20100509964010; "China and Russia Hold Consultations Between the Two Countries' Foreign Ministries," Xinhua Domestic Service, June 30, 2010, CPP20100630005003.

[102] "Medvedev Outlines Key Tasks for Russia's Far East in Khabarovsk Speech—Text," July 2, 2010, CEP20100704950102.

[103] Fiona Hill, "Dinner with Putin: Musings on the Politics of Modernization in Russia," Foreign Policy Trip Reports, No. 18, Brookings Institution, available at <www.brookings.edu/reports/2010/10_russia_putin_hill.aspx>; and Andreas Rinke, Reuters, "Beijing No Threat to Russia, Putin Says," *National Post*, September 7, 2010, available at <www.nationalpost.com/todays-paper/Beijing+threat+Russia+Putin+says/3487882/story.html>.

[104] "Medvedev: Russia-China Relations 'at Their Highest Point Now,'" *Rossiya* 24, September 28, 2010, CEP20100928950055.

[105] Aslund, Guriev, and Kuchins, 245.

[106] Qian Tong and Li Shijia with Han Jie, Li Zhongfa, and Liao Lei, "China Strategizes Major-Power Diplomacy and Embraces Global Cooperation in the 'Post-Crisis Era,'" Xinhua Domestic Service, May 24, 2010, CPP20100524636005.

[107] Aleksandr Khramchikhin, Deputy Director of the Institute for Political and Military Analysis, interviewed by Yuriy Kotenok in "A Nanoarmy for a Nanocountry," Segodnya.ru, July 10, 2010, CEP20100712358035.

[108] Edward Cody, "Russia to Aid NATO on Antimissile Network in Europe. Accord Signals New Era of U.S. Security Relations with Former Cold War Foe," *The Washington Post*, November 21, 2010.

[109] Phillip C. Saunders and Joshua K. Wiseman, "Buy, Build, or Steal: The PLAAF's Quest for Advanced Military Aviation Technologies," paper prepared for the 21st CAPS–RAND–CEIP–NDU Conference on the PLA, October 28–30, 2010, Taipei, Taiwan; and Stephen Blank, "New Strains Emerge in the Sino-Russian Military Relationship," *China Brief* 10, no. 1 (October 22, 2010).

[110] "Turkmenistan-China Gas Pipeline Put in Operation," ITAR–TASS, December 14, 2009, CEP20091214950079.

[111] Author's interviews with Russian analysts in Moscow, May 2010.

[112] Andrey Polunin, "China is Expanding: First Taiwan, Then Siberia and the Far East—PRC is Building Roads Along Russo-Chinese Border at an Accelerated Pace," *Svobodnaya Pressa*, June 28, 2010, CEP20100629041016.

[113] Simon Saradzhyan, "Russia's Diversionary Maneuver," *Zvezda Povolzhya*, June 3, 2010, CEP20100607358004.

[114] Dmitri Trenin, "U.S.-Russian Relations: How Does Russia See the Reset?" Carnegie Endowment for International Peace, October 28, 2009, available at <http://carnegieendowment.org/files/Full_Transcript%20of%20Event.pdf>.

[115] Konstantin Kosachev, "Yeshche raz ob eksporte prostranstva i mozgov," *Ekho Moskvy*, August 20, 2010, <http://echo.msk.ru/blog/kosachev/704720-echo/>.

[116] "Medvedev outlines key tasks for Russia's Far East in Khabarovsk speech."

[117] David Barboza, "China Passes Japan as Second-Largest Economy," *The New York Times*, August 16, 2010.

[118] Simon Saradzhyan, "Russia's Diversionary Maneuver," *Zvezda Povolzhya*, June 3, 2010, CEP20100607358004.

[119] Polunin.

[120] Saradzhyan.

[121] Aleksandr Khramchikhin in Aronov and Bazanova, "If There Is War Tomorrow," *The New Times*, February 22, 2010, CEP20100222358018; Khramchikhin in Yury Kotenok, "A Nanoarmy for a Nanocountry," Segodnya.Ru, July 10, 2010, CEP20100712358035.

[122] Fedor Lukyanov in Aronov and Bazanova, "If There Is War Tomorrow."

[123] Sun Yefei, "Game Playing Between Great Powers Behind Frequent Military Exercises in Northeast Asia," *Zhongguo Qingnian Bao*, July 9, 2010, CPP20100709788007; Mikhail Lukanin, "Military Reform Will Be Checked Out in 'Vostok,'" *Trud*, June 28, 2010, CEP20100628358012; Saradzhyan; Kotenok; Aleksandr Karasev, "A Summertime Exacerbation at Sea," Vladivostok, July 28, 2010, CEP20100729358001.

[124] Khramchikhin in Kotenok, "A Nanoarmy for a Nanocountry."

[125] Aleksandr Aladdin and Aleksandr Khramchikhin in Andrey Polunin; and Khramchikhin in Kotenok.

[126] Valery Usoltsev, "Combat at the Sergeyevskiy Range," *Suvorovskiy Natisk*, July 17, 2010, CEP20100719358011.

[127] Khramchikhin in Kotenok.

[128] Khramchikhin in Aronov and Bazanova; Saradzhyan.

[129] Dale Herspring, "Is Military Reform in Russia for 'Real'? Yes, But . . . " in Blank and Weitz, 151–191.

[130] Anatoly Tsyganok in Lukanin.

[131] Khramchikhin in Kotenok.

[132] Dmitry Gorenburg, "Vostok-2010: Another Step Forward for the Russian Military," July 19, 2010, available at <http://russiamil.wordpress.com/2010/07/19/vostok-2010-another-step-forward-for-the-russian-military/>.

[133] Cynthia Roberts, "Russia's BRICs Diplomacy: Rising Outsider with Dreams of an Insider," *Polity* 42, no. 1 (January 2010), 38–73; Michael A. Glosny, "China and the BRICs: A Real (but Limited) Partnership in a Unipolar World," *Polity* 42, no. 1 (January 2010), 100–129.

[134] "Apparent Text of 'Leaked' Draft of Russian Foreign Policy Document ["Program for the Effective Systemic Utilization of Foreign Policy Factors in Support of the Long-Term Development of the Russian Federation,"] and Accompanying Letter to President Medvedev from Foreign Minister S. Lavrov [dated February 10, 2010]," *Russkiy Newsweek Online*, May 11, 2010, CEP20100514037004.

[135] Peter Baker, "Obama Aims to Build Economic Ties with Russia," *The New York Times*, June 23, 2010.

[136] Yevgeny Satanovsky, "Opinions," *Izvestiya*, August 10, 2006, CEP20060810018002.

[137] Yevgeny Satanovsky, "Iran, the Once and Future Empire," *Izvestiya*, August 14, 2006, CEP20060814021001. See also Parker, 291.

[138] Viktor Litovkin, executive editor of the *Nezavisimoye Voyennoye Obozreniye* military magazine, told Ekho Moskvy, "The fact that we have a contract with Iran on the supply of S–300PMU-1 is also an open secret. Such a contract exists. Another question is that because of some political motives we are not currently supplying [it] or we have not yet managed to produce this battalion [Russ: division] or two battalions of these air defense missile systems and therefore we cannot supply [them]." Ekho Moskvy Radio, December 22, 2008, CEP20081222950246.

[139] Interview of Rosoboroneksport General Director Anatoly Isaykin by Vadim Soloyev, "Rosoboroneksport Strengthens Positions," *Nezavisimaya Gazeta*, February 4, 2009.

[140] Ariel Cohen, "Russia's Iran Policy: A Curveball for Obama," The Heritage Foundation, Backgrounder, No. 2359, January 15, 2010, 2. Cohen cites meetings with Putin and Lavrov in Moscow in September 2009. The present author heard other sources say much the same at a conference in Washington, DC, in early 2010.

[141] Author's interviews with Russian analysts in Moscow, May 2010.

[142] "Medvedev Speech to Envoys Notes 'Paradigm Shift in International Relations,' Transcript of speech delivered by Russian President Dmitry Medvedev at a conference with Russian ambassadors and permanent representatives to international organizations in Moscow on 12 July 2010 at 1700 hours," Russian Federation President Web site, July 12, 2010, CEP20100713009001.

[143] "Speech by Iranian President Mahmud Ahmadinezhad during a closing ceremony of the Iranian Youth Festival in Tehran," Islamic Republic of Iran News Network Television (IRINN), July 23, 2010, IAP20100724950093.

[144] Russian Federation Presidential Edict No. 1154 of 22 September 2010, "On Measures for the Fulfillment of UN Security Council Resolution 1929 of 9 July 2010," September 22, 2010, CEP20100922753001.

[145] Dmitri Trenin, "Russia Reborn: Reimagining Moscow's Foreign Policy," *Foreign Affairs* 88, no. 6 (November–December 2009), 77.

[146] Dmitri Trenin, presentation on "Russia's Foreign and Security Policy: An Update," Carnegie Endowment for International Peace, Washington, DC, September 17, 2010.

[147] Dmitri Trenin, "The Reset Has Begun," *The Moscow Times Online*, June 4, 2010, CEP20100604964009.

[148] Fyodor Lukyanov, "Strategic Triangle in Uncertain Environment: U.S.-China Relations as Seen Through the Russian Prism," paper presented at conference, *Impact of U.S.-China Relations in Asia: Regional Views, Woodrow Wilson International Center for Scholars*, Washington, DC, September 20, 2010.

[149] Fyodor Lukyanov, panel remarks delivered at conference, *Impact of U.S.-China Relations in Asia: Regional Views*.

[150] Sergei A. Karaganov, "The Past Year and the Upcoming Decade," February 15, 2010, available at <http://karaganov.ru/en/publications/preview/99>.

[151] Sergei Karaganov, "After the 'Reset,'" *Rossiyskaya Gazeta Online*, September 29, 2010, CEP20100929006001.

[152] But, in his view, there could be no strategic alliance between Russia and China. Author's interviews with Russian analysts in Moscow, May 2010.

[153] They include Japan, South Korea, Vietnam, Indonesia, and Australia. See, for example, John Pomfret, "Issues Remain as U.S.-China Talks End," *The Washington Post*, May 26, 2010; John Pomfret, "U.S. Continues Effort to Counter China," *The Washington Post*, July 23, 2010; Craig Whitlock, "Gates to Meet Chinese Counterpart in Hanoi," *The Washington Post*, October 6, 2010; and Mark Landler, Jim Yardley, and Michael Wines, "As China Rises, Wary Neighbors Form Alliances," *The New York Times*, October 31, 2010.

[154] See, for example, Marina Ottaway, "Iran, the United States, and the Gulf: The Elusive Regional Policy," Carnegie Papers, Middle East Program, Number 105, November 2009, Carnegie Endowment for International Peace, Washington, DC.

[155] See Lo, 157–195, for an excellent historical analysis of triangulation assertions and reality up to 2008, prior to the onset of the global economic crisis, and of five alternative scenarios for Russia-China relations in the future. Lo briefly hints at something akin to the tentative new paradigm described in the present paper in his discussion of the "strategic tension" scenario. There (p. 193) it appears as one of two possible Russian reactions to "strategic tension" with China: either persist in attempting to play the role of balancer between East and West, or "gravitate slowly back to Europe and become part of a larger Western consensus."

[156] For the roller-coaster story preceding the vote, see Edward Wong, "Differences in Priorities Drive Rift with China," *The New York Times*, February 20, 2010; Colum Lynch, "China Signals Shift on Iran Sanctions," *The Washington Post*, March 25, 2010; Mark Landler and Andrew Jacobs, "Strains Easing, Chinese Leader Plans U.S. Visit," *The New York Times*, April 2, 2010; John Pomfret,

"Out of an Intricate Dance, Improved U.S.-China Relations," *The Washington Post*, April 10, 2010; Mary Beth Sheridan and Scott Wilson, "Obama Presses for Unity on Iran," *The Washington Post*, April 13, 2010; and Colum Lynch, "Six Powers Discuss Iran Sanctions," *The Washington Post*, April 15, 2010.

[157] "Apparent Text of 'Leaked' Draft of Russian Foreign Policy Document."

[158] Author's interviews with Russian analysts in Moscow, May 2010; Fedor Lukyanov, "Loading Back," Gazeta.ru, August 19, 2010, CEP20100819041020.

About the Author

John W. Parker is a Senior Research Fellow in the Institute for National Strategic Studies at the National Defense University. He served previously in the U.S. Department of State's Bureau of Intelligence and Research, where he was Deputy Office Director and Chief of the Division for Caucasus and Central Asia in the Office for Russian and Eurasian Analysis. His principal areas of expertise are Russia and the states of the former Soviet Union and Russian-Iranian relations. He has served two tours at the American Embassy in Moscow, where he was Chief of the Political/Internal Section from 1989 to 1991, and was Deputy Director of the U.S. Information Agency's "Research and Development—USA" exhibit in the Soviet Union in 1972. Dr. Parker has also been a Public Policy Scholar at the Woodrow Wilson International Center for Scholars and a Guest Scholar at the Brookings Institution. He holds a Bachelor of Arts degree from Indiana University and a Ph.D. from Yale University.